The Grotta House by Richard Meier

Foreword by Richard Meier
Interview with the Grottas
Essays by Joseph Rykwert and David Revere McFadden
Photography by Scott Francis, Thomas Grotta
Edited and designed by Massimo Vignelli

The Grotta House by Richard Meier

RIZZOLI
NEW YORK

First published in the United States
of America in 2007 by
Rizzoli International Publications, Inc.
300 Park Avenue South
New York, NY 10010
www.rizzoliusa.com

ISBN-10: 0-8478-3009-8
ISBN-13: 978-08478-3009-1
LCCN: 2007920987

Cover: Photography by Scott Frances
End Paper: Photography by Scott Frances

Distributed to the U.S. trade by Random House, New York

Design: Massimo Vignelli
Design Production: Vignelli Associates

Printed and bound in China

2007 2008 2009 2010 2011/ 10 9 8 7 6 5 4 3 2 1

Photo Credits

Scott Frances: 2–3, 36–37, 38–39, 40, 41, 42, 43, 44–45, 46, 47,
48–49, 50, 51, 52–53, 54, 55, 56, 57, 58, 59, 60, 61, 62, 63, 64–65,
66–67, 68–69, 70–71, 98–99, 110–111, 118–119

Thomas Grotta: 16, 18, 23, 25, 73, 81, 82, 83, 84, 85, 86–87, 89, 90,
91, 92, 93, 94, 95, 96, 97, 100–101, 102, 103, 104, 105, 106, 107, 108,
109, 112, 113, 114, 115, 116–117

Content

Thank You

On September 8, 2005, we celebrated our fiftieth anniversary in our favorite place, our home. There will come a time when other people's personalities and possessions will transform our marriage with Richard Meier's architecture. By virtue of Richard's reputation, one facet of the house seems destined to remain the same: its name. Our home may always be known as the Grotta House, but it won't be the Grotta house as we know it. This book is our picture of the house as we see it, and a personal thank you note to the special people who designed it, built it, and filled it.

Architects
Richard Meier
Michael Palladino
Ralph Stern
David Ling

Landscape Architect
Walter Carell

Contractors
Phil and Larry Drill

Cabinetmakers
Gerry and Mario Laracca

Crafts Artists and Designers
Joyce and Edgar Anderson
Toshiko Takaezu
Mariette Rousseau Vermette
Many other favorites will become apparent
by their numerous appearances in the book

House Lifers
Accent Painting
Bob Snyder
Bryan MacArthur
Dan Tuck
Ed Moseley
Andy Kristofferson
Woody Drabik
Tony Nascimento
Guy, Dean, Marc Torsilieri
Seventeen years later they are still on our job.

Writers
David Revere McFadden
Joseph Rykwert
Thanks for so insightfully putting us in our place.

Photographers
Scott Frances
Tom Grotta
Scott's work keeps improving with age.
Tom Grotta can't improve with age: he's been perfect
since the day he was born.

Massimo Vignelli
Bravo to our maestro for your enthusiasm,
clarity, and unique vision. You're the only person
in the world capable of putting sheep on the cover
of a Richard Meier book.

Richard Meier
Last but not least, to our Don Quixote friend,
Richard: Thanks for the house.
And our compliments to the chef.

he creation of a house is a unique endeavor that charts a direct path to the most fundamental architectural principles and challenges. Every house demands clarity of expression, which for me has always involved the articulation of basic geometric forms. This geometry is the generating force for other, more complex elements and juxtapositions, of openness and closure, solid and void, opacity and transparency. And throughout the process of experimenting with and manipulating all of these formal and phenomenal relationships, one strives to achieve a sense of wholeness and completion that is at once lyrical and lucid, poetic and tangible. This is the case for any work of architecture, but these forces operate on an almost elemental level in the design of a house. Add to the basic, distilled nature of the type the caprices and dreams of the families one designs for, and the process achieves a depth and richness that goes a long way toward explaining the powerful influence that so many of these relatively small-scale projects have had on the development of architecture over centuries.

The house is an intimate architectural expression, and it requires a fearless conspiracy between architect and client that reveals first a set of desires and anxieties and later, one hopes, their harmonious realization in built form. From the beginning of the process of designing their house in rural New Jersey, Lou and Sandy Grotta had a strong sense of what they required. They were passionately involved clients from the outset. And the fact that Lou and I had known one another from childhood made communication more direct and perhaps simpler because of our shared history. From our very first discussions it was clear that their vast collection of craft objects and Sandy's extensive experience as an interior designer would be important in the design of the house. So one of the first goals was to reconcile the scale of the architecture with the scale of the objects and furniture to be displayed and arranged inside so that no one element was overwhelmed by any other. The sensitivity with which we all approached the task of integrating the Grottas' original collection with my design for the house produced an enduring harmony between an ever changing set of objects and the space they occupy.

The site for this house presented few limitations but did in fact, due to view, orientation, and the slope of the land, give clues to the organization of various spaces. Therefore the house's organization and geometry found expression in an unusually direct manner, a strategy that emerged from a need to impose order on the openness and freedom of the surrounding landscape. While other houses I have designed, notably the Smith and Douglas houses, are objects in their landscapes, the Grotta House operates more as an extension into the landscape, so that its strong formal geometry anchors the house to the site and is necessary to modulate the fluid relationship between interior and exterior spaces.

And while every commission I undertake is tailored to client and site, the constant preoccupation is with light. For centuries painters, sculptors, and architects have expressed the mood of their times through the qualities of light. But it is only relatively recently that architects have had access to large-scale glazed surfaces of superior quality. The Grotta House benefits from the presence of vast areas of transparency as much as any other structure I have designed. The goal here as in any project is the true experience of light as it evolves throughout the year. It is the experience of a mutable yet profound presence rather than a set of sensational effects or illusions. It is the essence of architecture.

Interview with the Grottas

hat were your homes like growing up?

Sandy Grotta I lived in a beautiful section of Detroit in a rambling country-style house my parents were forever redecorating. All our interiors had dark wood furniture and purportedly English antiques. It was like my mother, immaculately neat and very well dressed.

Lou Grotta Mine was a typical suburban, nondescript West Orange, New Jersey, home, decorated, in my mother's indecision, with an all pink master bedroom.

Where did you first meet?

L At the University of Michigan in 1953.

Describe your first home.

L It was a thirty-year-old center-hall colonial; its main attractions were its sensible layout, its proximity to grammar school, my sister's house, and our budget.

S It was beige, inside and out.

Did you both agree on how it should be furnished?

S I wanted it in the spirit of my parent's house only not as formal.

L I wanted modern, preferably Scandinavian.

S Our mediator was Lou's mother's decorator, who tastefully furnished it in a mixed bag of semi-forgettable furniture and accessories.

How did crafts come into your life?

S The Museum of Contemporary Crafts' 1957 "Furniture by Craftsmen" show introduced us to the wonderful work of Joyce and Edgar Anderson. Soon afterward we commissioned our first of many dark walnut Anderson pieces. The Andersons were to become our bridge to other craftsmen, the catalyst to my becoming our decorator, going to interior design school, and entering the field.

Sandy, what was your impact on your home?

S Over the next twenty years, I completely redid what we had previously done. All the moldings, drapes, and filigree went, as did the beige, brightened to white.

14

Our original furniture and accessories were slowly deaccessioned, replaced by wood, metal, fiber, and ceramics by contemporary craftsmen, architects, and designers. While a lot of our objects are purely sculptural, we've always had a love for great functional design: Toshiko Takaezu's tea bowls, Jack Lenor Larsen's fabrics, Arne Jacobsen's hollowware, Hans Wegner's chairs, Mies van der Rohe's sofas, and Richard Meier's house.

When did you become architecture junkies?
L Our first real eye openers were the art history courses we took together at Michigan. From then on wherever we've gone, when we're not hunting down crafts, we've hunted down architecture.

What was your criteria for selecting an architect?
S Years of working with local architects made me want to work with a world-class one at least once.

When and where did Richard Meier come into your life?
L Our families go back forever. Richard grew up in a bland, blend-into-the-neighborhood Maplewood home a few miles from mine. We went to Sunday school and camp in Maine together and were members of the same country club. During our high school years we often played basketball in his backyard. These games were marked not so much by the high quality of play but by the intensity of kidding that went on among its players. Richard was a man of few words but he could get a zinger in with the best of them. A far more talkative, occasional participant was Peter Eisenman. Among all the words of wisdom bandied back and forth, I don't recall anything discussed that in anyway had anything to do with the world of architecture. When I first saw Richard's parents' new house published, I must admit I was startled. From what I thought I knew of Meier's abilities, I would have thought his name was as likely to appear in the box score of the New York Knicks as in the architectural section of the New York Times.

The previous house.

For sandy · with best wishes for a very happy birthday · love ~ichael · 7 June 1999

Was Richard the only architect you considered?

L We interviewed one other major architect. We were impressed with his personality and credentials but uncomfortable with the likely extent of his participation. To him the Grotta house might seem a minor project; to us it was clearly the most important architectural undertaking since Stonehenge.

What was your history with Richard?

L After college, we saw a lot more of Richard in the media than we did in person. We closely followed his career and greatly admired his work, despite the fact that his material sense was obviously the opposite of ours, other than using wood floors. As for all his glass, glass was the only major craft media we never collected. We thought of Richard, not as a potential architect but as an old friend who might recommend someone for our job. On the way to his office Sandy nervously asked, "Suppose he says he would like to be our architect?" I eased her anxiety by quoting a recent interview Barbaralee Diamonstein had done with Richard in which he stated, "Quite honestly, I don't think I would do another house where I did not have complete control of the interior design." Following a few reminiscences in his pre-Getty-sized office, we laid out where we were coming from. After we finished, we were greatly surprised when Richard said he knew the right architect for us: Richard Meier. He then explained how he felt confident our two seemingly opposite agendas could work together without seriously compromising each other's vision. Frankly, we weren't totally comfortable with his conclusion but we were totally comfortable with him.

How specific were you about your requirements?

L When Richard visited the old house we showed him how we lived and the importance of our crafts. We requested, wherever possible, that he architecturally position our pieces so they could be seen from 360 degrees. Conversely, we wanted to make sure our home neither looked nor felt institutional. Other than spelling out a few pet peeves plus our storage and spatial requirements, we consciously tried not to tie his hands.

Was Richard involved with choosing the site?
L Very much so. As he said, "Many houses fail before starting out, stillborn from the site." It took months of looking and a couple of Meier vetoes before we found unobstructed land on the high ground of a New Vernon wheat field. To quote Richard, "There was no back facade, nothing to defend the house from, no worst view."

How was the design first presented to you?
L As a very small cardboard model with a few sketchy drawings.

What was your reaction?
L Shock. While we didn't know exactly what to expect, we never expected a classic Palladian-style rotunda. Once Richard explained its dynamics, its logic came into focus. While it was radically different in appearance, its relationships from room to room were very similar to our present home.

Was the design altered along the way?
L From the first model to final plans, the heart of the design stayed basically the same. The only major changes were our elimination of the swimming pool, backyard pavilion, and a large screened porch off the kitchen and dining room. Our budget drained the swimming pool. We never asked for the screened porch, nor did we like the thought of looking through one. Richard warned that living in horse country was bound to be buggy and suggested we test the waters by taking a few picnics. When we did and we weren't badly bitten, the porch bit the dust. As for the rear pavilion, we thought it a bit pretentious. Once we moved in and could see architecture wherever we looked, we realized its visual purpose. We later attempted to rectify the situation by planting a semi-circle of white birch trees after they served as the main decorative element for our daughter's wedding.

Did you have trouble finding a contractor up to the challenge presented by the house's design?

L The firms we initially interviewed were all house builders, few of whom could fully fathom our plans, much less had any desire to build them. Our first contractor quit after completing the foundation. His successor was a commercial contractor, Drill Construction, headed by Phil Drill, a sometime sculptor who welcomed the challenge. It helped greatly that there was an architect on Phil's staff, his nephew Larry.

What problems did you encounter during the construction process?

L Not having Drill's input from the beginning and their lack of previous experience with our architects was a definite handicap. We had our tribulations, trials, and a few errors but we finally assembled a team up to the challenge of Meier's unforgiving standards. If a second-rate orchestra tries to play Beethoven, you're headed for a headache. It took the ingenuity, determination, and skill of a special group of creative people to make our house sing.

You must have had conflicts between practicality and aesthetics?

S We did with our lighting. We had to choose between pin spotting specific objects or adhering to the grid of the ceiling. We chose the latter. From the beginning, we knew the living room presented morning sun problems. When we could not agree on a satisfactory shading solution, we decided to do without and covered the furniture with Sheila Hicks's Japanese paper blankets. In the morning our living room looked like a Christo creation. Finally, ten years later, we found a curved track from which strips of solar veil screening could successfully descend from our 22-foot ceiling.

Sandy, what was your role in the project?

S I served as the curator of its content, most of which came from the old house. We did commission some new Anderson furniture and bought a large number of Eames swivel chairs so we could easily see all around us.

18

What did the experience of building your house teach you?

L That we have a darn good marriage.

Did the architecture and the crafts work together?

L Aesthetically, yes, but in terms of collaboration, no. Richard did raise the possibility of designing furniture that the Andersons might build. We never asked them. We knew they had no interest in executing anyone else's idea.

Does your home work?

S My years of design experience served as a long dress rehearsal for our dream house. It might seem cold and demanding to others; for my particular way of living it works perfectly. As an example, most of our appliances, phones, and TVs are hidden in drawers or behind doors. People blame the inconvenience on the architects, but generally the architect isn't the culprit; the client is. What we love to look at looks best with a minimum of visual distraction.

What were the major differences living in your new home?

L We had read many architectural articles on the impact of natural light in Richard's projects. Until we lived in Richard's space, we couldn't appreciate its ever-changing magic.

S When visitors come after dark, Lou insists on putting on his light show. It starts with his turning off every light in the house. Even on a moonless night, once a person becomes acclimated, there is always enough natural light that they can easily move about without fear of breaking their necks. Richard's architecture doesn't stop at its four walls; it involves the total environment. On a clear night, the moon casts strong shadows over not only the interior walls but also the lawn outside. In Maplewood the only wildlife we saw was an occasional raccoon knocking over our garbage cans. We now live in the middle of a neighborhood of deer, wild turkeys, Canadian geese, horses, and sheep. When there's a lightning storm, it's like the 4th of July. During a snowstorm you get the sense of living in a snowglobe turned upside down.

Did you make any major changes once you moved in?

L Aside from changing the front door from wood to glass, our biggest alterations were outside. One can never anticipate the dramatic changes of scenery that other people's idea of architecture—and a heavy deer population—can create. We've planted many a tree to cover what the deer uncovered and what our neighbors introduced into the landscape.

What are some of the unexpected aspects of the house?

L We never realized the true dynamics of glass. Architectural photographers very often pump in artificial light to take out the reflection of the glass. As a consequence, most pictures of glass houses fail to present a true picture of what you actually see. During the day, when I'm outside looking in, our glass becomes a mirror that creates wonderful Magritte-like scenes. When I'm on the front lawn and Sandy's at her upstairs desk, she often looks as if she's sitting in the clouds behind me. Inside at night, the mirror reverses itself producing an entirely different but equally dramatic effect.

What questions do people most commonly ask?

L Did it come in on budget? Does it leak? Knowing what you know now, would you do it again? The house did exceed its budget. When we're asked to be specific, we answer that question with another question. What does it cost to stay in the most expensive penthouse in the best hotel? Multiply that by 365 times the seventeen years that we lived here. The answer is: our house is a bargain. Our budget excesses were as much voluntary as involuntary. Our biggest problem was five short words: "It would be nice if. . . ." Our architects were great at generating new ideas we couldn't refuse. As for leaks, we do our share of caulking; we have yet to experience any major internal water damage.

Would you do it over again?
Both Definitely.

What would you do differently?
L Hire a construction manager to interact between the contractor and the architect. Plan a bigger basement for the five grandchildren we didn't have at the time and, like everyone else, we could use a few more closets.

When did you take possession of the house and make it yours? Or does it always belong partially to Richard?
L When we first moved in, we were a little intimidated about changing anything. It didn't take long before that was no longer an issue. I will admit that to this day when we make a change we try to anticipate what he would think.

Has the house changed your collection?
S Only in its direction. Since our son, Tom, opened his fiber gallery in Connecticut, our emphasis has shifted to tapestries and baskets. As our photographs show, we like to move pieces around; one thing remains constant: wherever they're placed, their best is brought out by our ever-present natural light.

Is the house demanding?
S Yes, but it deserves to be.

You built the house after your children, Tom and Tracy, left. Did it become an adopted child?
S Only in the sense that we baby it.

Is it a friend?
S Next to my family, it's probably my biggest love.

Do you expect to always live in the house?
L It was designed with space for an elevator so that physical circumstance wouldn't force our leaving. Short of a sheriff's eviction, we're in for the duration.

Do you ever think of yourself as the house's caretaker and do you ever think about what will happen when you no longer own it?
L We know we're not in the position of an Edgar Kaufmann and Fallingwater. We would like the next owner to keep things as they are, but we realize that is unlikely. All we can do is record our experiences, leave the house in great condition, and cross our fingers that future owners will respect it as much as we do.

Do you think of your house as a legacy?
L We don't think in those terms, but obviously we're proud of it and hope our excitement about architecture is contagious.

Facing page:
Three plates by Peter Voulkos.

**W**hen Louis and Sandy Grotta decided to build a house on the site they had found in Harding Township, not far from their old home and their work, there was little hesitation about how to find the architect. Lou Grotta had grown up together with Richard Meier and they had remained friends. When they visited the site together, Meier immediately saw how the lay of the ground and the wooded hillside, which half-ringed it, could provide a perfect setting for a house. It was open towards the east and south, while the wooded hills to the north and west configured themselves into a kind of theatre from which the inhabitants of the house might look over the meadow and its life.

It was the beginning of a process which Antonio Averlino, a Florentine sculptor-architect known as Filarete, described about 1460 in his romanced architectural treatise: as any man who wants to have a child will need a woman to bear it, so anyone who wants to build will need an architect in whose mind he might plant the seed of the building, to be nurtured there much as a child is nurtured in the womb. The intimate process Filarete described is rare enough nowadays, but it does appear, however, that in the case of Sandy and Lou Grotta working with Richard Meier, a house was brought forth which answered the clients' every particular need. The program which the Grottas gave Meier and the site conditions together became the seed of his conception.

Meier took the hemicycle of the western woods as one half of a notional circle into which he inscribed a square. Where the diagonals of the square crossed each other, he set the center of the house. The sides of the square he sub-divided into sixteen modules—sixteen (the first cube on the first square) being Vitruvius' perfect number, though this perfection may only be coincidental. By subtracting one module from the whole square, Meier obtained the shifting diagonals on which the plan is elaborated. And he further divided each module into four sub-units. This last division gave him the dimension of the paving tiles which recur throughout the house, both in and out.

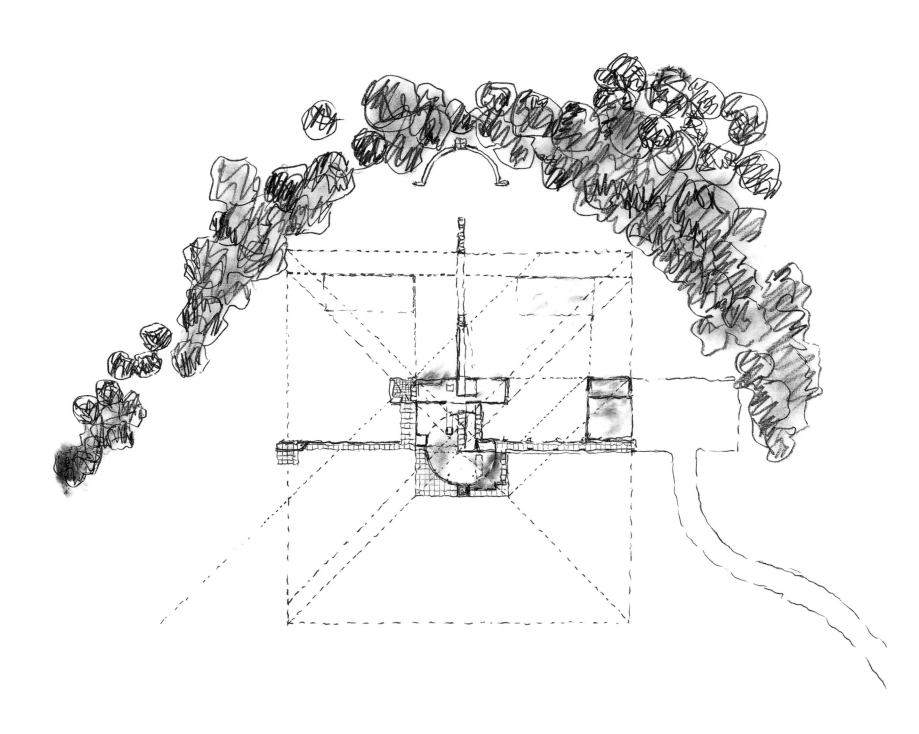

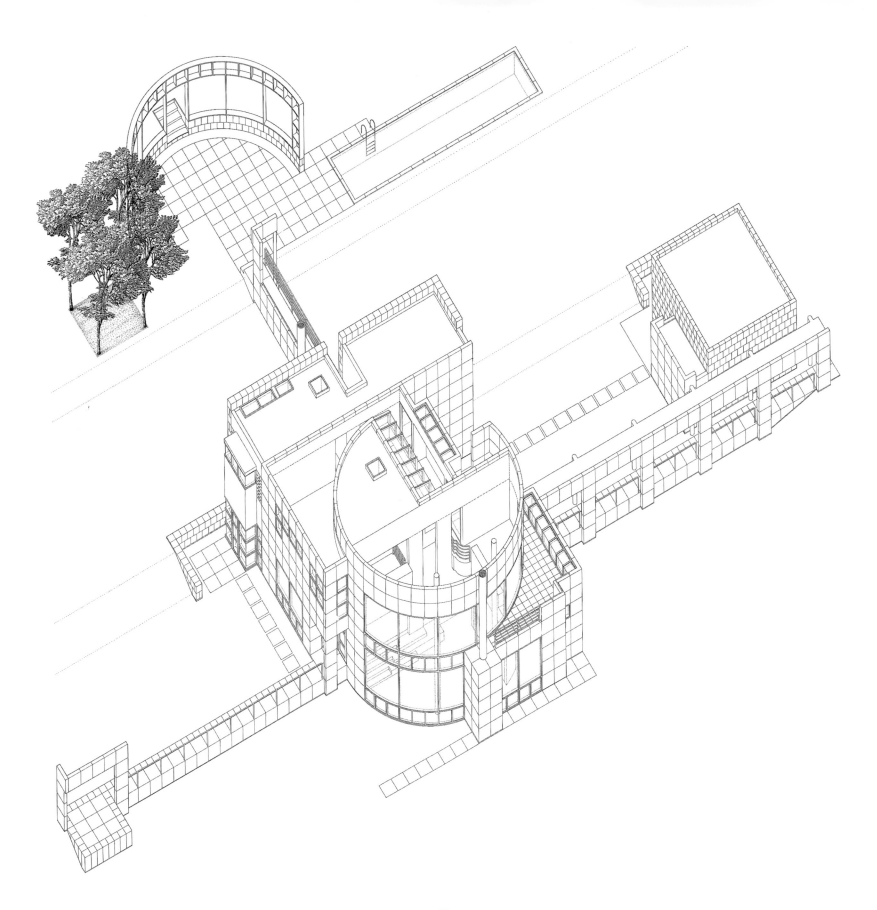

Such deceptively simple decisions, as well as his reliance on the formal elements which are part of his normal repertory have nevertheless led Meier to articulate a seemingly complex space. He has done this in part by playing odd against even numbers of the modules. The hub of the whole layout is a cylindrical volume, half of which is given over to the double-height living room. The rest of the plan was developed from a contrast between the cylinder and a rectangular block adjoining it, so that the geometry of the cylinder is articulated by (and married to) a net formed by the rectilineal layout which governs the rest of the house. This contrast in the geometries turns to a play of material surface and color on the outside of the house: the cylinder (as well as the exterior walkways) are sheathed in white enamel panels, the orthogonal parts are either in grey enamel or in darker grey ground-faced concrete blocks.

One way to take in the main articulation of the house — which is organized on a line running approximately from north to south—is to walk the whole length of that original (notional) square on which the plan is based. Where it meets the north edge, it is marked by the entry into a covered passage (backed by the carport), which acts as the porch that brings the visitor to the front door. As you pass through the door, you enter the body of the cylinder about which the house revolves. But the view through it allows you to look beyond—to the path which leads to a gazebo. That very airy gazebo marks the southern border of the built terrain.

On coming into the cylinder, you will find the necessary coat closet and services on your right—as well as a passage that gives access to the inner rooms; on your left, a wall allows you to read the implied presence of an inner sheltered room, which you will also have noted from the outside, but which you can enter only from the double-height living space; it provides a very useful display area for some of the extraordinary artifacts which Lou and Sandy Grotta have collected over many years.

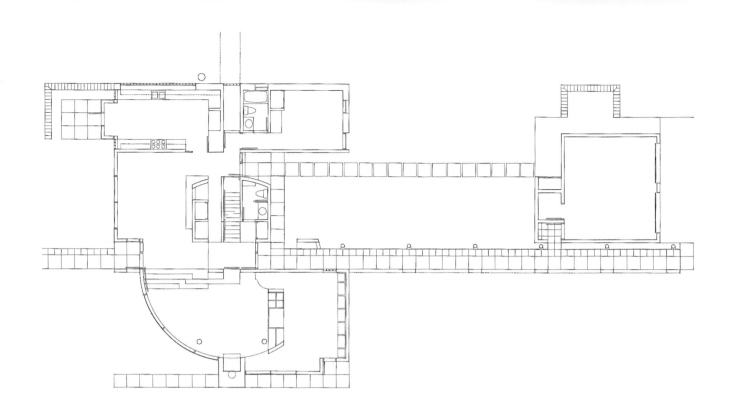

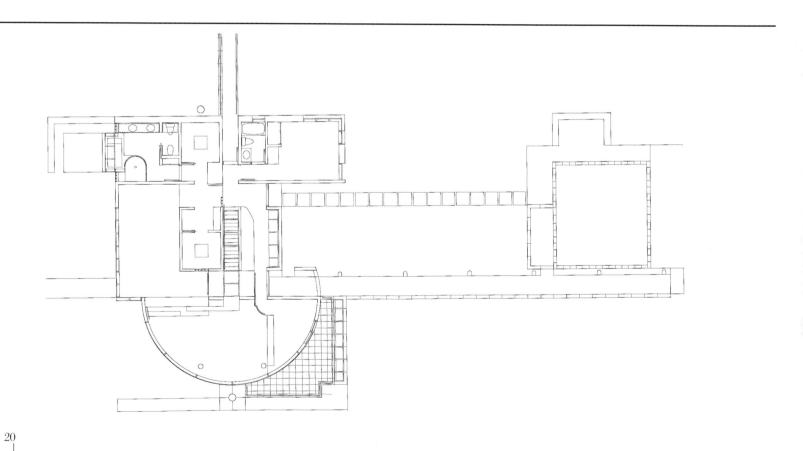

0 5 10   20

You can appreciate the open layout of the whole house once you find yourself inside the cylinder, since—when you look up—you see, on your right, the bedroom which opens into the double-height space as a balcony, while you will be aware of another balcony and railing behind you, that of the alcove over the sheltered closed gallery. However, the most important element is clearly the striking fireplace, set in a tall rectangular chimney piece (which measures two small 32 inch units square, a dimension that is rather crucial to the way the whole geometry of the plan is modulated). Both from within and without, it is obviously the heart of the house. The rectangular chimney breast rises the full height of the lower story and continues as a cylindrical flue at the upper floor level.

On this walk you will have noted that the line on which you entered also divides the double-height part of the room from the lower, more intimate rectangular dining area with a large kitchen beyond it. If you continue beyond the double-height cylinder, through the outer door, you will find yourself walking on the edge of a veranda which articulates the fall of the ground and ends in that gazebo which—in the original drawings—measured one module each way; though lying on the boundary, it is half in and half out of the enclosing diagram. It therefore offers a miniature of the geometry of the house, as if it were sounding its keynote.

Opposite the fireplace and at right angles to your passage through the house, a discreet stairway rises to the upper floor. As it rises, it continues out of the house through a sharply articulated slit to become a passerelle which meets the rising land in the background, set against the background of the encircling trees which give the house such a noble setting. The original project showed a semicircular screen, taking up the diameter of the focal cylinder and interposed between the house and the enclosing copse, but that and the swimming pool fell victim to later modifications, perhaps to the ultimate advantage of the house, which sits so well in the open meadow against its leafy background.

The stairway separates the two parts of the orthogonal layout of the house, which is not a simple dwelling, but also serves as the background to a unique collection of modern crafts: wood, fiber, and ceramics. The rooms need therefore to be considered as places where such pieces would feel as much at home as their human inhabitants. That depends above all on the ingenious filtering of the light, but also on their proportions and the use of level changes in the dark, almost black split—and therefore slightly craggy—slate floors.

The perceptive visitor will note how the floor is stepped near the entrance to become a podium for some of the larger, more monumental pieces, both fiber and ceramic, which sit well against the dark slate of the floor and can therefore be seen "in the round." At ground level, too, the semicircular double-height space is further articulated by that more sheltered rectangular room, a gallery ideal for displays—small, domestic. One wall of it is "readable" to the left of the entering visitor, as I have already suggested, but it is approached from the double-height sitting-room into which it intrudes—so that the cylinder, so striking on the exterior, only shows itself to the visitor as little more than a quadrant.

I already noted that the staircase divides the house into two. The passage from the dining room back to the entry hall passes under the stairs as a curved wall, which allows a fragment of the cylindrical geometry to peep through the orthogonal organization. The staircase can then go down another level, to the exercise and utility rooms in the semi-basement, which the fall of the site allows to become a "lower ground floor."

The division worked by the stairway in fact separates the two rectilinear areas at the main level: the dining room (which opens from the double-height space) with its kitchen on one side from the guestroom—and the return passage round to the entry spaces on the other. At the upper level, the bathroom and bedroom suite, which in turn opens back into the double-height cylindrical space is articulated from the other sequence. Across the landing from the bathroom is the library (which corresponds to the guestroom below), with its large west-facing picture window specifically designed as a background to one of the larger terracotta pieces. Corresponding to the bedroom suite is the long gallery wing in which some of the smaller sculptures and artifacts have their home, but with its long working table it is primarily Sandy Grotta's office. It projects into the double-height space as the alcove I also mentioned earlier. With its curved window looking to the south-east over a gentle fall of the meadow, this alcove opens onto a small terrace. It has become one of the Grottas' favorite most relaxing space in the house. The balustrade through which it opens into the double-height space runs at a right angle to that of the bedroom, so that while the layout of the house may seem tightly axial, the internal articulation of the volume is asymmetrical and playful.

The way the light is shrewdly modulated through the house is essential to the display of the collection but also integral to that playfulness: the large curved windows of the cylindrical living room which look east and southeast correspond to differentiated openings in other orthogonal walls, which are quite modest in places to allow the full effect of several top-lights, as in the staircase or in Sandy's office. The irregular, often rough or knobbly surface of many of the objects in the collection contrasts with the regular and smooth surface of the walls and plays against its very insistent patterning and the hardwood floor on the upper level.

Indeed, the Grottas have responded playfully to every lead Meier has given them; they have appropriated each part of the house—including the basement, which I have not mentioned, as it plays a minor part in the formal game—and used the house as if it really was the fruit of the kind of joint conception Filarete described.

And they have cherished their home—which is why it now seems to fit their way of life as a well-made glove might fit a hand. Playful but not arbitrary: I don't know why (apart from the rhyme) playful is often equated with willful. Yet play is anything but. On the contrary, games and play always involve rules. Of course, any such rules, however elaborate, have to be ingenious and flexible enough to allow players both invention and initiative. This is equally true of baseball and of chess—but also of the play of design, of architecture. Meier is a brilliant player in a game in which he has had to supply some of the rules himself as he has developed the elements of his formal method. He is one of the few architects in his generation who have deliberately set out to supply the discipline of design in the late twentieth and twenty-first centuries with both a method and a repertory of formal devices, some of them borrowed from the masters of previous generations as has been the practice in the past, but other elements are very much his own.

What the Grotta House shows very convincingly is that the method and the repertory can become part of that interplay between client and architect which Filarete called gestation—and can make the house something much more amenable than the proverbial machine for living in. I might even venture to suggest that the interplay of architect and client and the enmeshing of the passion for craft objects into this interplay gives the Grotta House a unique status among the American houses of recent decades.

Filarete's text in *Antonio Averlino detto il Filarete, Trattato di Architettura*, ed. by Liliana Grassi, Milan 1972. Book II is called "How a building is generated, analogously to the human body." I quote from page 39 ff.

Facing page:
Ceramic form by Toshiko Takaezu.

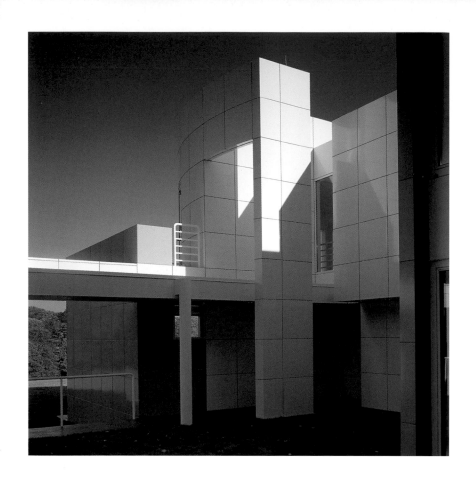

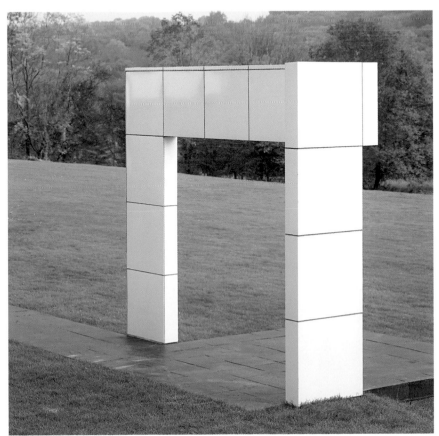

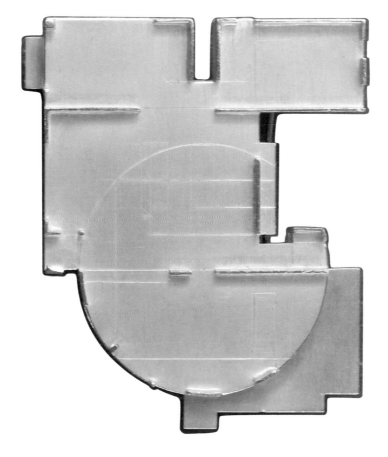

Michael Becker's House Broach

73

lthough written over two centuries ago, Goethe's commentary on the relationships between art and craft seem particularly pertinent to the role played by handcrafted objects in Sandy and Lou Grotta's home and life: "All arts begin with necessity. There is hardly a thing, among all those that we own or use, that we cannot fashion into a pleasant shape, position in a suitable place, and bring into a certain relationship with other things."

For more than five decades, craft has been integral to the collecting aesthetic of the Grottas. Distinctive furniture, vessels, and textiles, positioned in suitable places, and revealing relationships between objects and their setting are all central to the subtle yet seductive environment that is created in the Grotta House. Sandy and Lou Grotta did not set out to be collectors; rather they have furnished the extraordinary architectural environment in which they live with objects that give their daily lives both pleasure and meaning.

Objects made in the craft mediums—wood, fiber, clay, metal, glass—have a unique ability to link the past with the present. From the earliest days of human culture to the present, the knowledge and skills of the hand have been conjoined with artistic visions to produce objects that are at once beautiful and useful. In many instances, the beauty of an object can, in many instances, serve as its primary function.

In the Grotta House one encounters vases, bowls, baskets, chairs, textiles, and teapots, but also powerful sculptural forms, rich with an array of nature-derived or nature-inspired textures, colors, and shapes. Not only has the Grotta collection of craft been carefully and conscientiously assembled over the years, it is also a moveable feast; it is a living collection, and works of art shift their location and context as the collectors' tastes change, or as new work enters the collection over time. The collection has never been a static one; a ceramic vase that lives for a time in the downstairs den may find a new function in an upstairs bedroom. New combinations of color, texture, and shape needed to integrate a new acquisition into the home may require an entire rehanging and repositioning of the contents of a room. New relationships between space and object are constantly explored and tested. However, the guiding principle has always been to carefully consider the location of each object in relationship to the architectural environment. The goal is always to permit each object to live comfortably in its own space, without any artificiality or pretense. The collection grew as a result of what Joseph Rykwert, writing about the Grottas vision of architecture, called "deceptively simple decisions." It is in these deceptively simple decisions about what will be placed where that the quiet drama of the collection is revealed. Both Sandy and Lou have said that the objects they treasure and love to look at "look best with a minimum of visual distraction." Richard Meier's design gave them exactly the context the collection deserved.

It was in the mid-1950s that Sandy discovered the world of contemporary studio craft, and began a rigorous process of replacing family antiques with new work that reflected not only the spirit of the burgeoning American craft movement, but which suited the spare white modern interiors that appealed so powerfully to her. New Jersey furniture makers Edgar and Joyce Anderson became early favorites and dear friends of the Grottas. The Andersons are best known for the furniture they have designed for libraries, churches, synagogues, and for many private clients. For the Grottas the friendship they established with the Andersons became a preface to an extended family of artist/friends that have enriched their lives. In addition to revealing the eye of a perspicacious and disciplined collector, the craft collection is also an album of friendships that they have nurtured over decades.

If one makes an effort to analyze the formal elements of design that reverberate throughout the Grotta collection, four make themselves known immediately: the collection is ultimately about sculptural form; textures and surfaces that serve as visual foils to the planar white walls and expansive windows of the house are privileged; and the color palette of objects in the collection is derived from the materials from which they are fashioned —rich browns of roots and unglazed clays, the grays and blacks of natural fibers—but also blue, mauve, and rose that range from the evanescent morning-sky blue of William Wyman's glazes to an intense, almost Yves Klein, blue used with such grace by potter Toshiko Takaezu. Finally, throughout the collection one is constantly reminded of the presence of the human hand that brought the work into existence—the rough gouging and twisting of clay in hands of a Peter Voulkos, the subtle glimmer of Sheila Hicks' stainless steel and linen totem, or the intricate spiderweb knotting used by Rebecca Medel's cloudlike tapestry in the dining room.

Entering the Grotta House one is immediately struck by the vistas through the house that culminate in an imposing ceramic tree made by the Grotta's near neighbor and dear friend Toshiko Takaezu. Born of Japanese ancestry in Hawaii, Takaezu bridges the worlds of East and West in her swelling vessel forms. Sandy has chosen auspicious locations for each of the numerous vessels they own by giving each the opportunity to be viewed from a distance as well as in close-up. Another of the Grotta's favorite artists, John McQueen, uses a variety of natural materials—tree bark, roots, and vines—in his sculptures; a dramatic self-portrait made of spruce bark, positioned upside-down, greets the viewer at the end of another vista.

The hallway through which one approaches the living room and downstairs den is embellished with a superb horsehair wall sculpture by Dominic Di Mare. The son of a Sicilian-born fisherman and a crocheting mother, Di Mare uses natural fibers—frequently long strands of horsehair—to create floating sculptures that capture every delicate nuance of light and respond to any movement of air.

76

The living room is approached by way of slate steps, cleverly designed to serve as pedestals for a selection of baskets and fiber sculptures. On this diminutive amphitheater are displayed a deep blue reed and paper vessel by Mary Merkel Hess; the splayed fibers at the top suggest a waving field of cobalt wheat. Dorothy Gill Barnes, another of the Grotta's favored artists, is represented with three baskets that show her innovative and astonishing use of raw woods, barks, and vines. The siting of these works on the stairs echoes the intentions of the artist: when interviewed for the Archives of American Art of the Smithsonian Institution, Barnes said she hoped that people would not think of her work "as something you frame and put on the wall." Works by Gyongy Laky, Sheila Hicks, and John McQueen eloquently reveal the limitless artistic possibilities of fiber.

The one material that does not play a major role in the Grotta collection has been glass. It was only recently that the first major work in glass was added to the collection—a cast glass head by the Swedish artist and designer Bertil Vallien. Vallien is renowned for his powerful portrait heads that depict not a single individual, but which capture the essence of our shared humanity. This work adds not only visual contrast to the objects in the Grotta living room, but also serves as a subtle lighting fixture that casts a mysterious glow on the wall behind it.

The downstairs den celebrates the life and work of some of America's legendary ceramists. A collaborative work by potters Otto and Gertrud Natzler, who specialized in extraordinarily richly colored and textured glazes can be found here, as can an example of the subtle surface decoration and restrained glaze colors created by another husband and wife team of potters—Edwin and Mary Scheier. Three dramatic plates by Peter Voulkos are lined up to create a staccato rhythm on the wall, in front of which a coffee table made by Edgar and Joyce Anderson presents a hare-handled vessel by Ken Ferguson. Turner, like Takaezu and McQueen, is well represented in the

Grotta collection with a series of covered vessels and vases made at various times in the career of the artist. Another living legend—Lenore Tawney—is represented by a poignant linen tapestry titled "Morning Redness." Tawney's importance in the history of fiber art in the twentieth-century cannot be underestimated. Along with such major figures as Magdalena Abakanowicz of Poland, Tawney was instrumental in taking fiber off the wall and repositioning it as a primary medium for sculptors.

The viewer's attention in the dining room is drawn immediately to a wall-mounted planar sideboard by the Andersons, on which are a group of mysteriously timeless forms by ceramist William Wyman. A pyramidal piece in particular is typical of Wyman's ability to take simple and often geometric shapes and transform them with glaze into permanent watercolor landscapes. At one wall is a large multi-layered knotted fiber work by Rebecca Medel. In its complex layering the work suggests in infinity, as if one were looking through the architectural wall of the house into another realm. At the opposite wall a tapestry by Mariette Rousseau Vermette is also a metaphorical reference to infinity in its complex and rich texture and dreamlike colors.

As in many houses, the kitchen serves as a nerve center for the Grotta House. Hidden behind plain cupboard doors are impressive stacks of tablewares—plates, goblets, serving dishes—made by craftsmen from around the world. Sandy's love—after Lou, her family, and the collection—is great food. It is from this larder of vessels and utensils that Sandy composes table settings that reiterate her foundation principles of simplicity in design with elegance of material and craftsmanship.
For the Grotta's the line of distinction between art, craft, and design is subject to constant challenge. Nowhere is this better seen than in a lineup of tea and coffee pots that extends from one end of the kitchen to the other, designed or made by a range of artists that include architects Frank Gehry, Richard Meier, and Arne Jacobsen, designers Henning Koppel and

Russell Wright, as well as such studio artists as
Jim Makins, Nicolas Homoky, and Adrian Saxe.

The upstairs hallway is under the watchful eye of
Sheila Hicks' totem, mentioned earlier. Hicks has enjoyed
an international reputation since the late 1950s, and
has shown her work in museums around the world,
including Chile, Japan, France, Korea, Sweden, Israel,
and the United States, to mention only a few. Hicks'
work can be found in art collections that range from the
Metropolitan Museum of Art in New York to the
Centre Georges Pompidou in Paris and, of course, in the
Museum of Arts & Design.

Additional vessels by Toshiko Takaezu are composed on
the work surface used as a desk by Sandy. The design for
the house also included a sizable recessed display niche
that contains additional collections, specifically basketry
by the now familiar John McQueen, Dorothy Gill Barnes,
and Gyongy Laky. Making their first appearance in the
collection are other works by the late and much beloved
Ed Rossbach, by fiber and metal artist Mary Giles, and
Deborah Valoma.

Not all of the objects in the Grotta collection are abstract
studies in composition, color, texture, and form. Figural
studies and portraits have also engaged the Grottas
attention as collectors. In addition to the glass head
by Bertil Vallien in the living room, the "hand clock"
sculpture, a child's chair with embracing arms modeled
after Sandy herself (Sandy also figures as the model in
a knotted fiber portrait bust made by Norma Minkowitz
located in the downstairs den), and a figural vase by
Rudy Autio, one of the most expressive and colorful is a
large glazed dish by Viola Frey. Frey was a leader in the
San Francisco Bay area school of artists that adopted
craft mediums; she is known for her outsized ceramic
figures and also for her highly painterly platters.

Art in the master bedroom continues the themes of form,
texture, and color set out on the lower level. The space is

calming and meditative, and the art chosen to reiterate this theme. A long shelf holds a variety of turned wood vessels by Bob Stocksdale—subtle changes in profile, proportion, grain pattern, and form give this series an almost mantra-like presence. Over the course of his long career as a wood artist, Stocksdale brought the craft of lathe turning into the art studio, and set the tone for an entire generation of wood artists that followed him. A rocking chair by Sam Maloof, another living legend in the American craft movement invites the visitor to move into the room.

It is here that the Rudy Autio figural vase appears to stride forward into the space, on its way to a piled floor sculpture in figure made by Françoise Grossen. This installation gesture—using floors as well as walls and shelves rather than pedestals—gives the Grotta House a very special feel; the house remains a home, not an impersonal gallery with art lined up in formation.

How do all of these objects exist so happily with each other in the Grotta House? The basic principle is not far removed from the sentiment expressed by William Morris: "Have nothing in your house that you do not know to be useful or believe to be beautiful." Art, craft, and design live in the Grotta House on a daily basis. They are not appendages or afterthoughts. With their memorable forms and their tactile and engaging textures and colors, they speak eloquently about the creativity of the human hand, and the inseparable relationship of architecture and her sister arts.

Entrance Hall

The craft presence introduces itself as you enter.
On the previous page next to the front door,
a Wendell Castle walking stick and canes by (l to r)
Sam Maloof, Mira Nakashima, Markku Kosonen,
Edgar Anderson, Bob Stocksdale, and Norm Sartorius
rest in a Joseph Hoffman-designed stand.

John McQueen's upside-down spruce bark self-portrait
ends the progression from front to back door.
Richard Meier abstracted the door handle to the right
of the stairs from his design of the house.

Toshiko Takaezu's ceramic tree fronts the back hall
gallery whose niches display (l to r) the work of ceramic
legends Lucie Rie, Hans Coper, and Beatrice Wood.

Dominic Di Mare enlivens the hall further with two of his unique horsehair hangings.

Living Room

*On the previous spread, the slate steps descending to the
living room were designed to double as display platforms.*

(l to r) Mary Merkel-Hess's work of blue reed and paper.

*Gyongy Laky's open london plane tree piece held together
with electric wire.*

Sheila Hicks's piled linen construction "Garden de la Paix".

*John McQueen's structure (lower r) spells itself out
in aspen elm bark.*

The three other baskets were made by Dorothy Gill Barnes.

Facing page:
*A paper and kiyori thread sculpture by Naomi Kobayashi
faces four ceramic works by Toshiko Takaezu.*

Toshiko Takezu's classic forms rest atop Joyce and Edgar Anderson's coffee table. The opening in her moon pot was created naturally by the energy of the kiln.

Project architect David Ling designed the fireplace log holder.

Norma Minkowitz's woven bust of Sandy was a present from Lou.

Helena Hernmarck blueprint blanket came as her response to a request to create whatever she wished that related to the house.

Bertil Vallien's sandblasted glass head was electrified to light up the darkest corner of the room.

Edgar Anderson was the designer model and constructor of his walnut "hand" clock standing tall in the den.

Downstairs Den

Looking back towards the living room Paul Soldner's raku piece stands to the right of a Robert Turner mini-retrospective.

Lenore Tawney's linen manuscript tapestry "Morning Redness" hangs above Otto and Gertrud Natzler's bowl on the piano. The ceramic vessel to the right of the Anderson's bench is the work of Edwin and Mary Scheier.

One of Ken Ferguson's signature stoneware hares animates the Anderson coffee table beneath a trio of Peter Voulkos plates.

Dining Room

*Mariette Rousseau Vermette's tapestry hangs next to
Richard Notkin's stoneware head. Wendell Castle made
the profile table of birdseye maple veneer and mahogany.*

*Five William Wyman pottery pieces grace the Anderson's
floating server.*

*Don Lelooska's northwest coast frogfeast bowl crouches
across from Rebecca Medel's five-layered knotted linen
and cotton tapestry.*

*Sandy modeled the arms of the Anderson's grandmothers'
high chair.*

Kitchen

*Previous spread, in 1990 the kitchen was home to
Bill Wyman and Robert Turner's casseroles (upper l) and
a Karen Karnes bowl below. The walnut stools were done
by the Andersons. Pottery (from l to r) by James Lawton,
Mark Pharis, Mary Rohem, and William Wyman who
also did the lidded jar below next to a pair of Karen
Karnes. Sixteen years later a far different alignment
of international architects, craftsmen, and industrial
designers benefit from Richard Meier's special light.*

*This spread, top row (l to r): Amy Sabrina, Zhou Ding
Fang, James Makins, Toshiko Takaezu, Gustavo Perez,
Ronna Neuenschwander, Nicholas Homoky, Gerald and
Gottfried Weigel, Lu Wen Xia and Lu Jian Xing, Mark
Pharis, James Lawton, Adrian Saxe, Peter Voulkos.*

*Bottom row (l to r): Frank Gehry, Russel Wright,
Walter Gropius, Michael Graves, Richard Meier,
Henning Koppel, Arne Jacobsen.*

On big occasions the three dark Karen Karnes casseroles
and the five William Wyman's all get a good workout.

Charles Crowley's sterling silver chocolate server with
its wavy aluminum handle has yet to serve.

Strategically positioned at the head of the hall,
Sheila Hicks' seven-foot linen and stainless-tsteel thread
totem commands attention from all directions.

John McQueen's intertwined raspberry bush basket
looks out the den railing through the living room mullions
to the front lawn.

The built-in displays baskets by (l to r)
Ed Rossbach, Mary Giles, Dorothy Gill Barnes,
Norma Minkowitz, Dorothy Gill Barnes, Gyongy Laky,
Deborah Valoma, John McQueen.

Toshiko Takaezu ceramic forms corner a corner of the
desk in Sandy's office.

Lou's Den
*Ceramic plates by Viola Frey and Paul Soldner often
change places above the couch.*

Master Bedroom 1990
When Sugar and Spice took over this picture,
Wayne Higby and Bill Wyman's pottery sat on
the Anderson's dresser. The wood bowls were turned
by Bob Stocksdale. His wife Kay Sekamachi's paper
and fiber pieces rest on the near end table balancing
two ceramic forms by Toshiko Takaezu.

Master Bedroom

Sandy stores her jewelry in the Anderson's walnut chest of drawers. Mariette Rousseau Vermette's woven wool tapestry hangs to the right.

At this time, Bob Stocksdale's bowls surrounded ceramic pieces by Ruth Duckworth and Lucie Rie. His good friend, Sam Maloof, made the walnut rocker.

On the floor Francoise Grossen's heavy manila rope sculpture lies across from Rudy Autio's stoneware figure. Anderson's dresser now shows off work (l to r) by Dorothy Gill Barnes, Ken Ferguson, and Wayne Higby.

Bodil Manz's thin porcelain bowl and Ed Rossbach "hands on" basket presently occupy one of the end tables.

Library

The architects specifically designed the eight-foot-tall back window to frame William Wyman's ceramic and wood triangles.

In the hall behind Chief Don Lelooska's Staff, the glazed earthenware plate displays Robert Arneson in all his glory.

The collection on the library desk is ever evolving.
At this time it's inhabited by:
(upper row) Deborah Valoma, Ed Rossbach,
Ken Ferguson, Hans Weissflog, Wendy Ramshaw,
(second row) Bengt Berglund, Alexander Lichtveld,
Ken Ferguson, Bob Stocksdale, Lenore Tawney,
(third row) Bengt Berglund, Carmen Collell,
Bodil Manz, Tapio Wirkkala,
(fourth row) Marilyn Hank Otton, Toshiko Takaezu,
Karyl Sisson, David Gilhooly.

Index of Artists